LEO

SUN SIGN SERIES

ALSO BY JOANNA MARTINE WOOLFOLK

Sexual Astrology

Honeymoon for Life

The Only Astrology Book You'll Ever Need

LEO

SUN SIGN SERIES
JOANNA MARTINE WOOLFOLK

TAYLOR TRADE PUBLISHING
LANHAM • NEW YORK • BOULDER • TORONTO • PLYMOUTH, UK

Published by Taylor Trade Publishing
An imprint of The Rowman & Littlefield Publishing Group, Inc.
4501 Forbes Boulevard, Suite 200, Lanham, Maryland 20706
www.rlpgtrade.com

Estover Road, Plymouth PL6 7PY, United Kingdom

Distributed by National Book Network

British Library Cataloguing in Publication Information Available

Library of Congress Cataloging-in-Publication Data

Woolfolk, Joanna Martine.
   Leo / Joanna Martine Woolfolk.
      p. cm.—(Sun sign series)
   ISBN 978-1-58979-557-0 (pbk. : alk. paper)—ISBN 978-1-58979-532-7 (electronic)
   1. Leo (Astrology) I. Title.
   BF1727.35.W66 2011
   133.5'266—dc22   2011003083

∞™   The paper used in this publication meets the minimum requirements of American
National Standard for Information Sciences—Permanence of Paper for Printed Library
Materials, ANSI/NISO Z39.48-1992.

Printed in the United States of America

I dedicate this book to the memory of
William Woolfolk
whose wisdom continues to guide me,

and to
James Sgandurra
who made everything bloom again.

CONTENTS

ABOUT THE AUTHOR

Astrologer Joanna Martine Woolfolk has had a long career as an author, columnist, lecturer, and counselor. She has written the monthly horoscope for numerous magazines in the United States, Europe, and Latin America—among them *Marie Claire*, *Harper's Bazaar*, *Redbook*, *Self*, *YM*, *House Beautiful*, and *StarScroll International*. In addition to the best-selling *The Only Astrology Book You'll Ever Need*, Joanna is the author of *Sexual Astrology*, which has sold over a million copies worldwide, and *Astrology Source*, an interactive CD-ROM.

Joanna is a popular television and radio personality who has been interviewed by Barbara Walters, Regis Philbin, and Sally Jessy Raphael. She has appeared in a regular astrology segment on *New York Today* on NBC-TV and on *The Fairfield Exchange* on

CT Cable Channel 12, and she appears frequently on television and radio shows around the country. You can visit her website at www.joannamartinewoolfolk.com.

ACKNOWLEDGMENTS

Many people contribute to the creation of a book, some with ideas and editorial suggestions, and some unknowingly through their caring and love.

Among those who must know how much they helped is Jed Lyons, the elegant, erudite president of my publishers, the Rowman & Littlefield Publishing Group. Jed gave me the idea for this Sun Sign series, and I am grateful for his faith and encouragement.

Enormous gratitude also to Michael K. Dorr, my literary agent and dear friend, who has believed in me since we first met and continues to be my champion. I thank Michael for his sharp editor's eye and imbuing me with confidence.

Two people who don't know how much they give are my beloved sister and brother, Patricia G. Reynhout and Dr. John T. Galdamez. They sustain me with their unfailing devotion and support.

We are born at a given moment, in a given place, and like vintage years of wine, we have the qualities of the year and of the season in which we are born.

CARL GUSTAV JUNG

INTRODUCTION

When my publishers suggested I write a book devoted solely to Leo, I was thrilled. I've long wanted to concentrate exclusively on your wonderful sign. You are very special in the zodiac. Astrology teaches that Leo is the sign of love and luminous life-force. Your sign represents courage and confidence, creativity, abundance, and joy. You have tremendous charisma, an outer radiance that reflects your inner generosity and love of life. In essence, Leo symbolizes the concept of the *noble heart*. Especially you're known for your vitality and star-quality. Karmic teachers say you were picked to be a Leo because of your unusual boldness and valorous deeds in your previous life. But whether or not one believes in past lives, in *this* life you are Leo, dynamic superstar and great leader.

These days it has become fashionable to be a bit dismissive of Sun signs (the sign that the Sun was in at the time of your birth). Some people sniff that "everyone knows about Sun signs." They say the descriptions are too "cookie-cutter," too much like cardboard figures, too inclusive (how can every Leo be the same?).

Of course every Leo is not the same! And many of these differences are not only genetic and environmental, but differences in your *charts*. Another Leo would not necessarily have your Moon sign, or Venus sign, or Ascendant. However, these are factors to consider later—after you have studied your Sun sign. (In *The Only Astrology Book You'll Ever Need*, I cover in depth differences in charts: different Planets, Houses, Ascendants, etc.)

First and foremost, you are a Leo. This is the sign the Sun was traveling through at the time of your birth.* The Sun is our most powerful planet. (In astrological terms, the Sun is referred to as a planet even though technically it is a "luminary.") It gives us life, warmth, energy, and food. It is the force that sustains us on Earth. The Sun is also the most important and pervasive influence in your horoscope and in many ways determines how others see you. Your Sun sign governs your individuality, your distinctive style, and your drive to fulfill your goals.

Your sign of Leo symbolizes the role you are given to play in this life. It's as if at the moment of your birth you were pushed onstage into a drama called *This Is My Life*. In this drama, you are the starring actor—and Leo is the character you play. What aspects of this character are you going to project? The Leo optimism and courage? Its amazing creativity, magnanimous outlook, and generosity toward others? Or its boastfulness, pettiness, and narcissism? Your sign of Leo describes your journey through this life, for it is your task to evolve into a perfect Leo.

For each of us, the most interesting, most gripping subject is *self*. The longer I am an astrologer—which at this point is half my lifetime—the more I realize that what we all want to know is about ourselves. "Who am I?" you ask. You want to know what makes you tick, why you have such intense feelings, and whether others are also insecure. People ask me questions like "What kind of man

---

*From our viewpoint here on Earth, the Sun travels around the Earth once each year. Within the space of that year the Sun moves through all twelve signs of the zodiac, spending approximately one month in each sign.

should I look for?" "Why am I discontented with my job?" or "The woman I'm dating is a Scorpio; will we be happy together?" They ask me if they'll ever find true love and when they will get out of a period of sadness or fear or the heavy burden of problems. They ask about their path in life and how they can find more fulfillment.

So I continue to see that the reason astrology exists is to answer questions about you. Basically, it's all about *you*. Astrology has been described as a stairway leading into your deeper self. It holds out the promise that you do not have to pass through life reacting blindly to experience, that you can within limits direct your own destiny and in the process reach a truer self-understanding.

Astrologically, the place to begin the study of yourself is your Sun sign. In this book, you'll read about your many positive qualities as well as your Leo issues and negative inclinations. You'll find insights into your power and potentials, advice about love and sex, career guidance, health and diet tips, and information about myriads of objects, places, concepts, and things to which Leo is attached. You'll also find topics not usually included in other astrology books—such as how Leo fits in with Chinese astrology and with numerology.

Come with me on this exploration of the "infinite variety" (in Shakespeare's phrase) of being a Leo.

Joanna Martine Woolfolk
Stamford, Connecticut
June 2011

LEO

JULY 23–AUGUST 22

LEO MAJOR AND LEO MINOR.   Pl.20.

PART ONE

ALL ABOUT YOU

"The word impossible is not in my dictionary."

—Napoleon Bonaparte, a Leo

"Life is not about finding yourself. Life is about creating yourself."

—George Bernard Shaw, playwright and critic, a Leo

"I won't be happy until I'm as famous as God."

—Madonna, a Leo

"Life itself is the proper binge."

—Julia Child, chef and cookbook writer, a Leo

"Thank you, God, for this good life, and forgive us if we do not love it enough."

—Garrison Keillor, author, storyteller, and humorist, a Leo

"Fashions fade. Style is eternal."

—Yves Saint Laurent, fashion designer, a Leo

"To boldly go where no man has gone before."

—Gene Roddenberry, creator of *Star Trek*, a Leo

"Houston, the Eagle has landed."

—Neil Armstrong, astronaut and first human being to land on the moon, a Leo

YOUR LEO PERSONALITY

....

YOUR MOST LIKEABLE TRAIT: Exuberance

....

The bright side of Leo: Creative, magnanimous, colorful, cheerful, fun-loving, broad-minded

The dark side of Leo: Self-centered, conceited, self-indulgent, overbearing, bullying

Leo the Lion was born with regal instincts—you have a majestic quality. You're a magnet for people's attention and a charismatic performer. Your extroverted personality eagerly embraces life and you rush headlong into experiences that promise adventure. You are enthusiastic and generous, highly expressive, ambitious and flamboyant. You create an aura around you of glamour and excitement—and have a fund of energy that others draw on. Pride that tips easily into vanity is a marked characteristic. Its positive side is you can create splendid work you're proud of; its negative is you're extremely egocentric. Because your focus is on self, you can be oblivious to others' needs and wants. Your high-powered energy doesn't stop long enough to be sensitive to what another is feeling. Paradoxically, you're both bighearted and selfish.

All Leos possess a kingdom. The kingdom may be big or small; it may be your home or a lover or a piece of creative work or your whole career. But whatever it is, you are unquestioningly ruler of this kingdom. You don't have to look for a role to play in life—you've found it. You are the monarch.

Self-assurance surrounds Leo people like a ghost image on a television set. While others wait in the wings, you bask in the spotlight. Whatever you do, you do with a flair for the dramatic—everything about you is theatrical. This is not to say you're affected or insincere. Absolutely not. Your feelings and emotions are honest. The theatricality is your grand sense of style.

When you enter a room, you secretly hope everyone will stand up and sing a few stanzas of the "Hallelujah Chorus"! At a party, it isn't long before you assume control of the evening. Certainly, there's a shrinking Leo violet somewhere, but you're not noted for shy, retiring ways. You're a *sunflower*, not a wallflower—there's nothing backward or wishy-washy about you. Witty, vivacious, a fluent talker, you're a born entertainer who can lend spice to any occasion. You have a natural instinct for getting attention; people gravitate to you as steel filings to a magnet. Your energy is electric, trailing you like sparklers.

Because your nature is flamboyant and expansive, you despise the humdrum, the ordinary, and the dull. When real life does not supply all the excitement you need, you try to invent your own. You're the superstar of self-created drama, master of the grand gesture. To you, hyperbole is second nature. You never do things by halves—you do things in a r-r-really big way.

Leo symbolizes *pleasure*—you're fond of good food, fine clothes, elegant surroundings, and being treated as if you were rich and famous. Because they were born under the most royal sign of the zodiac, there's absolutely nothing Leo people can think of that's too good for them. Others may become reconciled to accepting second-best; not you. Luxury is as vital to you as breathing, and never mind what it costs. You're not a good haggler or bargainer because basically you want what you want when you want it. Leos are the most lavish spenders in the zodiac. (Librans run a close second.)

Your public image is very important to you. When a Leo woman's checking account is down to two figures, somehow she'll find the means to buy a glorious new dress. And when Leo man's credit cards are overdrawn, he will still make reservations at the best restaurant in town. If you invite people to your castle (which is how you think of your home), you entertain them royally. You're a splendid host.

Generous, kind, and openhearted, you find it hard to believe ill of others. Obviously, this is one of your most endearing traits. If injured, you will strike back quickly, but you also forgive easily and never hold a grudge. Marvelously affectionate and cheerful, you have genuine *joie de vivre*. Astrologers call Leos eternal children, for you take enjoyment from the moment and are uninhibited in giving affection. Whatever life dishes out, you retain an exuberant, looking-forward attitude. You're intensely *alive*.

The Sun is your ruler, and in many ways you're like the Sun itself—life enhancing, radiating energy and magnetism, burning with steady fixity. No one could ask for a better friend. If approached in the right way (flattery is the right way), you will do almost anything, but you expect praise and appreciation and admiration in return. Pride is your Achilles' heel, and vanity your weakness. Your ego demands not respect but adoration, not compliments but flattery. (If flattery were candy, you would eat it.)

When you receive lavish praise, you never stop to wonder if it's insincere.

In business, you naturally assume a position of authority. Another sign that gravitates toward taking command is Capricorn, but its natives steadily climb toward high position. Leos simply assume that they were born to it. One of your most useful assets in career is an unerring sixth sense for getting along with people who are in a position to be helpful. You know the value of socializing and, because you have a talent for inspiring others to do their best, work very well in group enterprises. You definitely have the skill to manage people and projects and to influence the lives of those around you.

Yes, you're controlling, but at your best you direct that control into constructive channels and positive plans. It's also true you're an order giver, not an order taker, but you're usually so cheery and enthusiastic that others don't mind taking orders from you.

Certainly no one works harder than you when your emotions connect you to a job. You never ask more of anyone else than you do of yourself. You won't quail before a challenge or flinch from confrontation. You will do the thing that scares you because to do otherwise spells failure to your eyes. You're ambitious, but not ruthless. All you ask is to be in the limelight.

You're especially drawn to the worlds of politics and entertainment. Fashion, music, theater, and the performing arts call to you. The world's a stage to you, and you were born with a "showbiz" personality.

Among your most striking characteristics is a refusal to be hampered by petty rules—nor can you be tied down to a task you consider tedious. You consider yourself above this, and some definitely call you too brash and arrogant. You can get high and mighty and quite condescending, and you do lean toward being a braggadocio. You try to top others—your stories must be funnier, your winnings bigger, your ideas more impressive—and you're unwilling to listen. You can easily slip into becoming the type of Leo whose grandiose plans evaporate as soon as the cocktail-party chatter ends. It's accurate to say you can be highly self-centered.

Indeed, your intense focus on self is an emotional burden you put on yourself. You take yourself far too seriously, and your craving for compliments causes you pain. Often, because you're too proud to ask for appreciation, you suffer silently from a wounded ego. Yet you seldom develop the self-detachment you need.

Nor do you ride out depression well. You're a Fixed Fire sign, and you define yourself by your goals and ambitions. When you're disappointed, you can become obsessed. If your efforts become blocked, you find it hard to change course. You hold on too long and get stuck in old patterns. The fire goes out, and you turn dark and brooding. Beneath your high-spirited bonhomie, you can be a tense and anxious overachiever with a nagging fear of failure.

Still, it is difficult (though not impossible) to dislike a Leo. True, you can be bombastic and overbearing. True, you love to give advice and at times are imperious about telling others what's best for them. Like your symbol, the Lion, you can be quite indolent, lethargic, and downright lazy; you like to sit back and bask in your own glory. But beneath your sometimes overweening self-assurance beats a caring heart—your hidden secret is you *need* to be needed. You can be accused of trying to run other people's lives, but the truth is you want to be involved. And your great warmth and sunny disposition are very hard to resist. The world would be much less fun without Leos.

THE INNER YOU

You have larger-than-life emotions. Whether you're experiencing joy, despair, excitement, or love, it might as well be playing on a giant movie screen. You feel you have an important role to play in life, and you're going to find it. You need to be involved in the world; in fact, you tend to think of any plan or project that you're part of as an extension of who you are. You believe in taking action. Your immediate reaction to a problem is to *do* something about it rather than sit around pondering it. This is not to say you always feel completely in control. Indeed, you're extremely sensitive, and you try to hide this fact under a lot of bravado. It's very important to you to get others' approval. In turn, when others need you, your first instinct is to offer help, advice, time, and effort. What makes you really special, though, is that in spite of your inner qualms, you jut out your chin and walk head-on into any challenge. You have a deep-seated need to prove your worth—not to others but to yourself. You'll tackle any job just so you can say, "I wasn't afraid to try!"

HOW OTHERS SEE YOU

You have a regal quality, a way of standing out in a crowd. The unique combination of the excitement you project, your sense of style, your way of speaking, and your laugh is what draws people to you. They're also seduced by the fact that you think big, which feeds their own fantasies of success and power. They're attracted to your energy and enthusiasm and your take-charge attitude. They assume you'll take a leadership position. But some people dislike what they consider your king-size ego. They think you hog the spotlight and that you're performing even when you're perfectly serious and sincere; they question your sincerity. Others regard you as a show-off who merely talks a big game. And there are those who think you have the temperament of a demanding, spoiled child.

GUARD AGAINST: Hogging the Spotlight and Being a Braggart

Your need to achieve is very deep, and so is the need to show off your successes to the world. In a sense, your life is a version of the childhood game of Show and Tell—you're continually showing and telling and demanding praise.

This tends to work against you. As you try overhard to project an image of self-assurance and pride, this translates into a message to others of "I am superior"—not a formula for gaining applause and winning support.

Plus you have thin skin for any kind of disapproval and absolutely hate criticism, which turns people off. They have to tiptoe around your touchy ego. In addition, you have no idea what objective self-criticism is. (It is *not* beating yourself up.) A better word is *self-assessment*—being able to accurately appraise your performance to learn what is superlative and what can be improved.

At your core, of course, you're trying to assuage feelings of *insecurity*—which coupled with your narcissism is a lethal combination. On the one hand, you fear you're not enough (talented enough, brilliant enough). You set high standards for yourself (almost impossibly high), and the fear of failure lurks in dark corners.

On the other hand, you feel you're the greatest—and one of your deepest inner fears is the universe will shortchange you by not recognizing how special you are.

The secret to vanquishing the fear, Leo, is to focus on work you truly love. When you're able to pour your energies into creating and accomplishing because of the *work*—not the accolades you think it will win—you will learn to take pride in yourself (which is totally different from egocentricity), regardless of your achievements.

YOUR GREATEST CHALLENGE: To Direct Your Leo "Magnificence" into Something That Is Genuinely Magnificent

Ruled by the Sun, you like people to orbit around you. You can be a show-off, and it's very sad when you have nothing worthy to show off. Your biggest cosmic challenge is your pride—your life-long challenge of taking pride in the true creativity and genius of what you *do*, and not simply in self-aggrandizement. You have big needs (for applause, respect, love, attention), and your lesson is to be deserving of that attention. To fuel a sense of self-importance, you simply keep busy. You seek stimulation from the outside. You're restless, highly charged, immersed in projects and social activities. You're a classic Type A personality who keeps barreling on, fueled by an inner drive. (Leo is the sign of the heart, and your ferocious activity can put you at risk of a heart attack.) You're impatient with tedious detail, slow thinkers, and dreary, ordinary people. You demand immediate gratification, and when the action stops you become frantic.

Yet you don't need all this compulsive busyness. You were born to do larger feats and achieve greater accomplishments. You have masterful gifts of imagination, one-of-a-kind creativity, dynamic power to lead and influence, and a way of lifting the level of joy for everyone around you. You can dream big dreams and make them happen. Born under the sign of the hero, you can do great deeds that come out of your true power to create, not out of your self-centered need to exalt yourself. Indeed, the key, Leo, is to get out of *yourself*, get out of your ego. Focus your magnificence and brilliance on ventures and relationships of greater meaning.

YOUR ALTER EGO

Astrology gives us many tools in our lives to help manage our struggles and solve problems. One of these tools is to reach into your opposite sign in the zodiac—your polarity.

For you, Leo, this is Aquarius, sign of hopes, wishes, and aspirations. Aquarians are noted for seeing the big picture, for their detachment, and for going their own way. Conversely, Leo tends to be caught up in the current drama. You're strongly involved with others, and you focus on making a brilliant impression. Even as a child, you would choose role models and practice imitating them so that your friends would see you as important and interesting. Because it's so crucial that you be viewed as a winner, every mishap (a snub from someone you counted on, a deal falling through) is a personal blow. Acknowledgment, recognition, and applause are overly important, which causes you grief.

Aquarius is a visionary who looks toward future possibility and concentrates on freedom of expression. Aquarians are idealistic, independent, and in love with liberty. As a sign, it's certainly more mental than emotional. Love tends to be more impersonal—it takes a humanitarian approach and is concerned with social justice. Aquarius wants to express its own individuality, and it matters not if its opinions are unpopular. For many Aquarians, the focus is to free themselves from tightly controlled bonds, difficult relationships, messy emotions, and petty bickering.

By tapping into Aquarius's above-the-fray attitude, you, Leo, can spare yourself the moment-to-moment misery you feel when you don't get the attention you deserve or people behave badly toward you. This Aquarius propensity to detach is not a *negation* of your feelings but a conscious practice of rising above the current disappointment or argument or obstacle in getting what you want. Instead of being sucked into a downward spiral in which you take everything personally, you can put your Leo energy into what truly will fulfill and satisfy. When you get past the emotional static, you can create and accomplish what you were born to achieve.

In turn, Aquarius can learn from you how to reach deeper into its heart. You forge strong links with others, and your magnanimous spirit of giving makes your relationships vibrant and intensely felt. Your attachments are profoundly life-enriching—without them, your soul would shrivel up. And surely, Aquarius could benefit from being as buoyant and upbeat as you, for this power of optimism actually brings success. You were born knowing The Secret—that positive thinking brings positive results!

LEO IN LOVE

You fall in love the way you do everything else—with grand and dazzling display. You're a high-spirited romantic whose glamour and *joie de vivre* make a love affair seem magical. Leo is the sign of the heart, of love and pleasure, and it can be rightly said that you invented romance.

You see love in practically mythic terms. To you, a love affair is never minor or mild or murky. It is high drama; it is grand passion. The one who wins your favor moves instantly to center stage and radiates in the bright circle of your admiration. You praise your lover to the skies and adore giving presents. Generous, passionate, and vibrantly sensual, you know how to make every moment special. No one else in the zodiac can so easily make it seem that you two are the first, original, quintessential lovers. Certainly, having you as a lover is a heady experience!

Then, all too often, the lights suddenly dim, the curtain falls, the play is over—and you don't quite know what turned you off so quickly. It seems that, for you, falling out of love is as simple as falling out of bed. However, it's not this simple. You do indeed invest yourself totally in your relationships. But the reason you can be so quickly disillusioned is that the falling in love was about *you*. Love was a narcissistic reflection.

You want your world to be picture-perfect and your lover to be the fantasy of everyone else. Your feelings revolve around yourself: your goals, dreams, ambitions—and your ego. You mentally create a person who mirrors your view, then pour out your offerings to this wonderful, special lover you've "made up." It's in your Leo nature anyway to be over-the-top, and your love affairs are to a large extent self-created. You believe your extravagant movie story.

Often, you need the *experience* more than you need the actual lover—who is only the vehicle for you to feel the magic and ecstasy. Then when the real person supersedes the myth you've created, you're hit by the cold water of reality. In your Leo journey to maturity, it's important for you to see how you helped create the disillusionment by refusing to look at what was there at the beginning of the relationship.

Another reason for scales falling from your eyes is not receiving enough attention. You love to sun yourself in the light of a lover's total focus. You want someone who'll cater to your whims, ignore your shortcomings (you don't really think you have any), and dwell on your virtues. In the same way applause makes the star of a play seem larger than life, the lavish admiration of a lover makes you feel plugged into a life-enhancing incandescence.

Of course, you don't see yourself as demanding. You think you're openhearted and trusting, asking only what you give so generously: praise and affection. It's in your nature not to hold anything back, and, by the same token, you expect your chosen mate to be just as fervid as you are. If told you sometimes ask too much of those close to you, you simply don't understand how.

Another thing that causes you to back away from a relationship is if your lover makes you feel you're in competition with others. As far as you're concerned, you're the center around whom others orbit. The mere suggestion that the object of your affection may be looking at other objects of affection turns you icy. To begin with, you cannot bear disloyalty, and, second, you're completely turned off by competition. You're above that sort of rivalry, and actually are a little afraid of it. You can't be a loser, and one way to avoid being a loser is not to get into the race.

Still, although you won't put up with another's roving eye, you love to flirt. If you're a Leo woman, you send out subtle signals (you're too much of a blue-blood lady to be overt) that have men lusting after you. Leo male tends to be a Lothario, and at the very least adores the feeling that tons of women have a crush on him.

A further reason for a failed relationship is that living with you is somewhat overwhelming—and it may be a *lover* that does the detaching. It's not easy being attendant to a monarch, and you can be quite tyrannical. Sometimes a love partner will just call it quits to get out from under your control.

A worst-case scenario is if you marry someone you can dominate completely. In this relationship you may get total submission, but that is too little compensation for not getting the full, deep, robust kind of love you need. When you feel shortchanged in love, you will turn bitter and carping.

Happily, however, Leo is the sign that seems most emotionally healthy in love. You're also marvelously sensual, although kinky variations are not your game. You prefer to heighten and dramatize your lovemaking by being totally *involved*. You give full rein to your passion.

Despite the challenges of being in a relationship with you, you have truly royal gifts to offer. You are romantic to the core, and you invest your entire self in love. Indeed, your great strength as a person is your willingness to love. You're able to express feelings that spring from your honest heart. When a lover becomes central in your life, you give all your devotion. Your loyalty is unshakable. You'll fight for the one you love, defend him or her against all criticism. You're capable of making enormous sacrifice. No one burns as steadfastly.

Granted, in the "things to put up with" department, you are ego driven and have a constant need to impress; you're fond of bragging and exaggerating; your behavior can be outrageous; and you're domineering and demanding.

But when your mane is rubbed the right way, Leo the Lion is a genuine life enhancer. You're a divinely affectionate, cheerful companion with a sunny disposition and an optimistic outlook on life. Underneath your surface majesty is a sensitive, vulnerable person who needs reassurance. Of course you need applause, attention, devotion—you need what you give.

In love, you never look back and wonder whether you should have done this or that. You simply follow your heart, trusting that love will show the way.

TIPS FOR THOSE WHO WANT TO ATTRACT LEO

You can always win over anyone born under this sign if you show by your actions, your attention, and your unceasing compliments that you are completely and hopelessly lost in admiration. If you really feel this way, you're in clover. If you don't: fake it. Leos won't suspect your sincerity because they think they're fully as wonderful as you tell them they are. Leos almost never think compliments go too far.

There is another way to make an impression on Leo: Be funny. They have a fine sense of humor and love to be entertained. (Didn't every monarch have a court jester?)

You can't go wrong attending a cultural event, especially a preview of some kind. Accompany Leo to a cocktail party that marks the opening of a new art gallery, an advance movie screening, or a lecture by an author about his or her forthcoming book.

Pet peeve for Leo men: Heavy makeup on women.

Pet peeve for Leo women: A tightwad date.

Bear in mind that both male and female Leos think the best is none too good for them. Leo travels first class. If you're trying to impress a Leo woman, take the rubber band off your bankroll, never wince at a restaurant check, get the best orchestra seats, and don't overlook the flowers, champagne, and telephone calls.

If you're trying to impress a Leo male, get the best cut of steak from the butcher and don't spare the wine. If he brings a good bottle of wine (and he will), exclaim over the astute choice he made, then exclaim again over the wine's bouquet and taste. And then bring out your final surprise—that flaming dessert or special after-dinner brandy.

Keep the ambience posh.

LEO'S EROGENOUS ZONES: Tips for Those with a Leo Lover

Our bodies are very sensitive to the touch of another human being. The special language of touching is understood on a level more basic than speech. Each sign is linked to certain zones and areas of the body that are especially receptive and can receive sexual messages through touch. Many books and manuals have been written about lovemaking, but few pay attention to the unique knowledge of erogenous zones supplied by astrology. You can use astrology to become a better, more sensitive lover.

For Leo, the back and spine are especially receptive to erotic stimuli. Sweeping caresses over this area of the body sexually stimulate and excite Leo. An easy and enjoyable preliminary to lovemaking is to sponge Leo's back in the bath with a loofah. Work gently down along the spine, pausing in the small of the back, then circle out to the sides and the ribs. Sponge until Leo's skin is rosy.

In the bedroom, while Leo lies on his or her stomach, shake talcum powder over the back (still tingling from the bath). Using your hands or a soft bristle brush, smooth the powder into the skin, paying particular attention to the spine and small of the back. Your Leo will be more than ready for love.

There are as many different kinds of back massages as there are masseurs, for this is an area in which tensions seem to gather. This technique will relax and soothe a Leo. Place the heels of your hands on Leo's upper back with your thumbs resting directly over the spine. Using a circular vibrating motion, describe six-inch circles with the heels of your hands. Trace a path from the shoulder blades down to the small of the back. Return. Repeat until the entire back has been massaged.

If you find this relaxes Leo so much that he or she falls asleep, erotically stimulate the back. Lightly draw long lines from shoulder to buttocks with your fingertip or fingernail just barely touching flesh. Stroke down into the cleft between the buttocks. Leo will wake up fast.

In general, don't pass up any opportunity to lightly touch your Leo's back. While passing by your Leo in a room or strolling together outdoors, give him or her an affectionate stroke on the back. This psychologically reassures Leo that he or she is loved.

LEO'S AMOROUS COMBINATIONS: YOUR LOVE PARTNERS

LEO AND ARIES

You two are the superstars of the zodiac. You're adventurous and communicative, and you live life at a pace that would exhaust most people. You get along marvelously in the bedroom—Leo and Aries are an unbeatable combination for deriving sheer joy and excitement from sex. You also share the same likes and dislikes in other areas. You're a red-hot couple who are great at thinking up new plans for socializing and travel, and have a large audience of adoring, admiring fans and friends. You both share "grand illusions" and enjoy spending money, and happily you two are also good at making money. However, you need all that rapport to overcome one big problem—the head-on collision of two super egos, each of whom want to play the leading role. You have to learn to share center stage. Otherwise, a glorious mating.

LEO AND TAURUS

Your Leo sovereign right to rule runs smack up against Taurus's determination to have its own way. Both Leo and Taurus are Fixed signs, so neither of you will give an inch. Leo merely becomes angrier and Taurus more obstinate. To start with, Leo is much more exuberant than Taurus, both in and out of the bedroom. Also, thrifty Taurus is appalled at your careless Leo spending habits. Taurus is cautious and deliberate and seeks security—while you're expansive and extravagant and want to live on a grand scale. As a couple, you arouse each other's resentments, for both of you are controlling. (Leo wants submission and adoration—Taurus wants final say in decision making.) The nail in the coffin is that Taurus stubbornly refuses to give you constant worship, and you're too self-centered to give Taurus the devotion it needs. Too many personality conflicts here.

LEO AND GEMINI

You strike it off immediately because you like so many of the same things—glamorous social life, parties, theater, lots of friends. The Leo-Gemini pairing is a combination of a generous, bighearted kid (you) and a lively charmer (Gemini). Active, independent Gemini brings out your Leo *joie de vivre*. Your affair is a merry chase after variety and amusement, and your shared adventures will be a bit of a whirlwind. It's very positive that you're both able to communicate. Also, you find Gemini's imaginative sexual high jinks great fun, though you may also become jealous because of Gemini's lighthearted approach to love. Gemini is far more laissez-faire than you—you're more intense than airy Gemini. Life together will be stimulating and exasperating, but the outlook is good if Gemini can stay faithful. Otherwise—poof!

LEO AND CANCER

Both of you are romantics, though in different ways: You want a relationship to be glorious and exciting; Cancer wants it to be meaningful and fulfilling. Cancer has a tendency to draw you into its sticky emotional web whereas you just want to assume your natural place on the throne. You don't get as overwrought as Cancer, who takes things more seriously. Cancer needs security and tranquility and is a stay-at-home. You're a boisterous gadabout who loves to be on constant display. Financially, your styles are totally different—you're a spender and Cancer is a saver. Still, emotionally you can find common ground. Cancer's dependency will please you, provided a little adoration is thrown in. You are flamboyant and passionate in love, and Cancer is responsive, loyal, and intense; you like this. Mixed signals.

LEO AND LEO

When a king and queen are together, heads turn. You two can have a royal mating—a grand passion conducted on a grand scale. You both are romantic, colorful, exuberant about life, and highly sexed. The erotic fireworks you set off in the bedroom only add to your beautifully matched energies in other areas of life—socially, in your careers, and in your big ambitions. Together you're a flamboyant couple who live lavishly, entertain regally, and travel stylishly. The main question is, who is going to be in charge? You're both determined to be splendid and admired, and it's difficult for one Leo to make room for another ego as large as its own. But this is exactly what's needed here. Each of you not only wants to sit on the throne, each wants to be the power behind it as well. Grand lovers and interesting rivals.

LEO AND VIRGO

You are drawn to Virgo's intellectualism, but Virgo doesn't understand your dramatic nature. You want romance to be magnificent and magical, and you cannot get from cool, reserved Virgo the sexual responsiveness you demand. Virgo's idea of compatibility is to agree on goals, lifestyle, and finances. Virgo is practical and prudent, conservative, frugal, and a nitpicker. Conversely, you are extravagant and a spendthrift, and like to live life in a really big way. Everything about Virgo puts a damper on your high spirits. Virgo has a way of looking at problems and seeing the downside first. You try to ignore the negative, which Virgo calls living in denial. Virgo won't be dominated, either. You need lots of flattery, but Virgo's nature is to be critical and puncture inflated egos. Both of you should look elsewhere.

LEO AND LIBRA

Your creative side meshes well with Libra's penchant for artistic and aesthetic pursuits. And romantically you're perfect together, for you both adore fantasy and high drama. You're more interested in the strictly physical side of love than Libra, but your style and brio can win Libra over. Libra is a very willing sexual experimenter. Libra does tend to be indecisive in life, and you'll naturally take charge. However, you can be imperious, which puts Libra on its high horse because it wants an equal partnership. Still, fair-minded Libra is willing to compromise. The checkbook may not always balance because both of you are extravagant and love a beautiful setting in which to shine. Each will also try to outdo the other in order to get attention. But in the bedroom, you're the reigning monarch—and that's what you like.

LEO AND SCORPIO

Both of you are passionate and sensual, and there is immediate sexual fascination with each other. But you find it hard to cope with Scorpio's jealousy and possessiveness. Intense, smoldering Scorpio is on a too-short fuse, while you are much more buoyant. You think Scorpio difficult and temperamental; Scorpio considers you a show-off. Indeed, you're perfectly ready to believe everyone adores you whereas Scorpio is emotionally guarded. Scorpio's drive is for control and security while it hides a complicated inner world of desire and distrust. Scorpio is not in tune with your fondness for a lavish lifestyle, and certainly doesn't understand why you have to be continually surrounded by an admiring audience. Scorpio would rather dominate than admire, and that doesn't suit your Leo penchant for being king or queen. Sex isn't everything.

LEO AND SAGITTARIUS

You are enthralled by optimistic, extroverted Sagittarius, and fun-loving Sagittarius is enchanted with your sunny openness and expansive outlook. Together you share a liking for freedom, exploration, and meeting new people. As a duo, you combine creativity, adventurism, assertiveness, and a restless striving to extract as much as possible from life. You have common interests as far as projects, plans, and career pursuits go. Sexually, you really shine, for Leo and Sagittarius are both passionate and fiery types who enjoy the erotic conflagration. You communicate wonderfully—erotically and otherwise—and if anyone can keep Sagittarius faithful, it's you. Your natural quality of leadership brings out what loyalty Sagittarius can give. You are very proud, but self-confident Sagittarius is perfectly happy to let you strut.

LEO AND CAPRICORN

Your romantic, expansive nature is curbed by cautious, practical Capricorn. You're a merry, fun-loving Leo who likes to kick up your heels, but Capricorn disapproves of too much self-indulgence. Capricorn's drive is to gain respect for its achievements, whereas you want to be admired just because you're magnificent. In this relationship you play the socialite, Capricorn the hermit. Both of you are highly sexed, but with basic differences. Capricorn is lusty but not romantic, and you need glamour in lovemaking, which Capricorn can't supply. You think Capricorn stingy with affection because Capricorn's reserved, undemonstrative nature cannot give you the adoration you need. Neither of you will take a backseat or let the other dominate. This affair will be on the rocks before it even leaves the dock.

LEO AND AQUARIUS

Leo and Aquarius are opposites in the zodiac—and the huge difference between you two is that you follow your heart, and Aquarius the head. Of course, like magnets, there's initial sexual attraction (a combination of physical desire and mental curiosity). Aquarius is drawn to your dazzle and exuberance, and you're intrigued by Aquarius's brilliance. But Aquarius's tendency to analyze and criticize will shake your confidence and deflate your ego. You view Aquarius's aloof emotions as a personal rejection. Also, Aquarius's unconventional, experimental approach to sex may prove upsetting—you don't like to wander too far afield. You both like socializing and meeting new people, but Leo needs to perform on center stage, which makes Aquarius impatient and irritable. Aquarius is too independent to become your devoted subject. And that's where it ends.

LEO AND PISCES

Leo is flamboyant and domineering; Pisces is unworldly and mystical. You intrigue each other because you are so different, but the differences don't mesh well. Your active, outgoing nature doesn't harmonize with Pisces's dreamy introspection. You need public acclaim, while Pisces prefers the sheltered life. You both have big dreams, but you want to be out in the world achieving your goals, whereas Pisces wants to withdraw and create. Each of you is more inclined to take than to give, and you can't tolerate Pisces's ultra-sensitivity. Pisces is far more subject to mood swings than you and, in communicating, neither of you tends to "hear" the other. Sexually, too, you're on different wavelengths—you want exuberant lovemaking, but Pisces's way of soul melding is through exotica. Before long, the Lion will start to roar.

YOUR LEO CAREER PATH

Security is far less important than being emotionally plugged into what you do, so it's important you find work that expresses who you *are*. You need labors that give you meaning, a lofty goal, a sense that you're a creator (not a cog). Mediocrity is not a Leo thing; the ordinary and commonplace depress you. If you don't feel you're doing something special—and *you* are special—your spirits quickly sink. If the job causes real unhappiness (it's too confining, too repetitive, too demeaning), it can literally make you ill. Leo is the sign of the heart, and your heart shrivels when it's not joyous. Other signs might do what they hate just for the money, but this would take a terrible toll on you. Therefore, it's important that you do something you love. Remember, Leo represents the themes of love and joy.

You're also goal-oriented, so another thing is to be clear about your objectives. Yours is a Fixed sign—when you take hold of something concrete, you make astonishing progress. It's when you're confused about a direction that your Leo energy is dissipated and your ambition seeps away. Allow your Leo fixity to keep you focused. You're definitely a workhorse in your power to produce *work*—though you're always the showiest racehorse out in front.

Speaking of showy, Leo is magnetically drawn to the flamboyant, glamorous, and valuable. Your work often involves products and services that have a luxurious flair. Also, your efforts tend to end up being lucrative.

You need an audience. Whether you're a bold Leo or the more secretly shy type, you're a performer. Something in you ignites in front of people—everything about you has heightened energy. With visibility you're at your best; recognition makes you feel good about yourself and moves you right past any private stage-fright. You're capable of achieving great fame in the public arena, and moving up into a "kingly" position just comes naturally.

Be careful, however, not to choose work that requires you to be on *all* the time. As it is, you put a lot of pressure on yourself, and the extra strain of constantly being in a goldfish bowl with all eyes on you is often too much of a burden. You need a balance between your public and private selves, and require alone time to invent and create.

Work that has big challenges brings out the best in you. No matter how much acclaim you get from others, it's truly your own approval that means the most. You feel the deepest pride in yourself when you've had to work hard for what you gain.

You have organizing ability, a gift for revving up people's spirits, and are an inspiring leader. This means you often find yourself in situations you instinctively know how to take charge of. Many a time a Leo who hasn't sought the top position is suddenly thrust there because others want the confident-*seeming* one to take the lead.

When you were growing up you loved playtime; you were exhilarated by games and using your imagination. Keep in mind that creative work brings out this spontaneous child-within. Also, a career with an element of risk-taking and gambling for high stakes taps into your adventurous Leo proclivities. Reaching for the brass ring—and then snatching it—adds to self-empowerment.

The real secret of your success is your spectacular ability to deal with people. You're a magician in person-to-person encounters, and so irresistibly likeable that others simply can't say no.

With your dramatic personality, the field of entertainment naturally calls to you. As has been said before, you have awesome star-quality. You also do well in sales, fashion design, interior decorating, public relations, and advertising. And being a born leader, you get high marks in any management or executive position. Politics, too, is an arena for which you're well suited. You can touch people's hearts.

Indeed, your *heart* is the key to being a happy Leo. You must do work that comes from your heart, expresses your passions, and emphasizes your exuberant nature. You love to have fun, and when your career brings you joy, you've found heaven on earth!

LEO AND HEALTH: ADVICE FROM ASTROLOGY

For optimum health, Leo must practice self-control, a word you tend not to understand. You love a larger-than-life life, which means you reach out for everything. You overindulge in eating, keep late hours, run yourself ragged. Your strength itself is your weakness because you're strong enough to push yourself to the limit. As the sign of the heart, Leo has a particular vulnerability to sustained stress causing heart ailments. Moderation is the key to your good health. You need to develop nutritious eating habits and find a good balance of exercise and recreation. You may not slow down but you certainly must have regular periods of rest. Stay centered and aware, and you will avoid the wild ups and downs of energy and mood to which Leos are prone.

Advice and useful tips about health are among the most important kinds of information that astrology provides. Health and well-being are of paramount concern to human beings. Love, money, or career takes second place, for without good health we cannot enjoy anything in life.

Astrology and medicine have had a long marriage. Hippocrates (born around 460 B.C.), the Greek philosopher and physician who is considered the father of medicine, said, "A physician without a knowledge of astrology has no right to call himself a physician." Indeed, up until the eighteenth century, the study of astrology and its relationship to the body was very much a part of a doctor's training. When a patient became ill, a chart was immediately drawn up. This guided the doctor in both diagnosis and treatment, for the chart would tell when the crisis would come and what medicine would help. Of course, modern Western doctors no longer use astrology to treat illness. However, astrology can still be a useful tool in helping to understand and maintain our physical well-being.

THE PART OF THE BODY RULED BY LEO

Each sign of the zodiac governs a specific part of the body. These associations date back to the beginning of astrology. Curiously, the part of the body that a sign rules is in some ways the strongest and in other ways the weakest area for natives of that sign.

Your sign of Leo rules the spine, the back, and the heart. The heart is associated with warm emotions, the back with courage. You display these qualities. You're an open, outgoing person who gives of yourself wholeheartedly to others and lives life to the fullest. In general, Leos have robust constitutions, supple spines, and good coordination. You're likely an excellent dancer and athlete.

As a Leo you need to excel in what you do. Often you push yourself so hard that you suffer strain from overexertion and nerves. You also tend to keep late hours and stint on getting enough sleep. Your upper back tires more easily than other parts of your body. You're subject to pains and pressure in your chest and around the heart. When you're startled, your heart seems to jump into your throat. You can usually feel your pulse beat inside your head. Leo is definitely noted for its longevity but later in life heart issues may crop up.

Your ruler, the Sun, has always been associated with the heart, back, and spinal column. It also influences the spleen and the entire body's vitality. In more recent times, astrologers have come to believe that the Sun rules the thymus, an endocrine gland that secretes hormones necessary for growth during the early years of childhood. Scientific studies connect the thymus with the immunization of the body against bacteria.

Thus, your sign of Leo is characterized by growth, vitality, and good health. You're not inclined to be sickly, and when you are ill you bounce back very quickly. As a rule, Leos live healthy lives. However, you must learn to slow down in later years to avoid any risk of heart attack.

DIET AND HEALTH TIPS FOR LEO

You enjoy the good life, and eating well is part of this. You're fond of rich food and fine wine. Fortunately, young Leo has a strong stomach and good circulation, and you keep in shape because you're active. However, time does catch up with you, and you must learn to eat correctly and cut down on fatty foods.

The cell salt* for Leo is magnesium phosphate, which keeps the motor nerves in top functioning order and is also necessary to

*Cell salts (also known as tissue salts) are mineral compounds found in human tissue cells. These minerals are the only substances our cells cannot produce by themselves. The life of cells is relatively short, and the creation of new cells depends on the presence of these minerals.

the formation of the skeletal structure. It forms blood albumin (a protein in blood plasma), maintains the fluidity of the blood, and activates the digestive enzymes. Foods that contain this element so important to Leo are whole wheat and rye products, almonds, walnuts, sunflower seeds, figs, lemons, apples, peaches, coconut, rice, seafood, beets, asparagus, romaine, and egg yolk. Foods that aid the circulation and have blood-making properties include beef, lamp, poultry, liver, fresh fruit, salad greens, cheese, whole milk, and yogurt. Foods rich in iron, such as spinach, raisins, and dates, are recommended for Leo. Plums, pears, and oranges reduce heart strain.

You should take care of your back by doing simple strengthening exercises. Learn how to bend and lift correctly, and never lift anything too heavy. You benefit from developing good posture, getting enough rest and relaxation, and enjoying short periods of sunbathing. (Always use sunscreen!)

Leos usually have thick shining hair, somewhat like manes. If you keep your hair clean, healthy, and conditioned, it should last you a lifetime.

THE DECANATES AND CUSPS OF LEO

Decanate and *cusp* are astrological terms that subdivide your Sun sign. These subdivisions further define and emphasize certain qualities and character traits of your Sun sign Leo.

WHAT IS A DECANATE?

Each astrological sign is divided into three parts, and each part is called a *decanate* or a *decan* (the terms are used interchangeably).

The word comes from the Greek word *dekanoi*, meaning "ten days apart." The Greeks took their word from the Egyptians, who divided their year into 360 days.* The Egyptian year had twelve months of thirty days each, and each month was further divided into three sections of ten days each. It was these ten-day sections that the Greeks called *dekanoi*.

Astrology still divides the zodiac into decanates. There are twelve signs in the zodiac, and each sign is divided into three decanates. You might picture each decanate as a room. You were

---

*The Egyptians soon found out that a 360-day year was inaccurate, and so added on five extra days. These were feast days and holidays, and not counted as real days.

born in the sign of Leo, which consists of three rooms (decanates). In which room of Leo were you born?

The zodiac is a 360-degree circle. Each decanate is ten degrees of that circle, or about ten days long, since the Sun moves through the zodiac at approximately the rate of one degree per day. (This is not exact, because not all of our months contain thirty days.)

The decanate of a sign does not change the basic characteristics of that sign, but it does refine and individualize the sign's general characteristics. If you were born, say, in the second decanate of Leo, it does not change the fact you are Leo. It does indicate that you have somewhat special characteristics, different from those of Leo people born in the first decanate or the third decanate.

Finally, each decanate has a specific planetary ruler, sometimes called a subruler because it does not usurp the overall rulership of your sign. The subruler can only enhance and add to the distinct characteristics of your decanate. For example, your entire sign of Leo is ruled by the Sun, but the second decanate of Leo is subruled by Jupiter. The influence of Jupiter, the subruler, combines with the overall authority of the Sun to make the second decanate of Leo unlike any other in the zodiac.

FIRST DECANATE OF LEO

July 23 through August 1

Keyword: Self-expression

Constellation: Ursa Minor, the Small Bear. This is the constellation of the Little Dipper. The Small Bear symbolizes goals and true direction.

Planetary subruler: The Sun

The Sun is both your ruler and subruler, and you are doubly under its beneficent influence. You enjoy being in the spotlight and may be known as a colorful personality. You have an artistic flair. You also have a knack for drawing attention because of the way you speak and present yourself. The role of a leader comes easily, for you are able to excite and stimulate others. In general, you don't keep your feelings to yourself. When you are happy, the world knows about it. When you are melancholy, you are usually vocal in expressing your moods. You are impulsive in love and tend to follow the dictates of your heart without thinking. At times, you can be very stubborn about wanting your own way.

SECOND DECANATE OF LEO

August 2 through August 12
Keyword: Expansion
Constellation: Ursa Major, the Great Bear. This is the constellation
    of the Big Dipper. The Great Bear symbolizes wisdom.
Planetary subruler: Jupiter

The expansive planet Jupiter corules your decanate with Leo's Sun, accenting intellectual and visionary qualities. You have a very proud nature and a quick temper. Your ability to dissect problems and see immediately what needs to be done gives you an authority that others respond to. Though you are jovial and good-humored, it's hard for you to laugh at yourself. You are ambitious, but not just for money; what you want is to know more, to gain in intelligence. While you can do manual labor, you much prefer mental pursuits. Sometimes you are thought of as being brash and overconfident, but this is simply a genuine expression of your enthusiasm and willingness to try.

THIRD DECANATE OF LEO

August 13 through August 22
Keyword: Creativity
Constellation: Hydra, the Water Serpent, who symbolizes activism and mental energy.
Planetary subruler: Mars

The aggressive planet Mars combines with Leo's Sun to underline your impetuousness and willpower. You plunge into new projects with verve, but you want tangible results for your efforts. Day-to-day routine quickly bores you; you need fresh ideas, new stimulation, and challenge to keep you at your best. Your life is often marked by furious bursts of energy, followed by periods of complete lethargy. In personal relationships, people are never in doubt about where they stand with you. Love may be troublesome because you want it to be perfect and you can be too demanding of a lover. You find waiting very difficult. Since you are outspoken, you dislike secretive people. Sometimes you have a reputation for being temperamental.

A *cusp* is the point at which a new astrological sign begins.* Thus, the cusp of Leo means the point at which Leo begins. (The word comes from the Latin word *cuspis*, meaning "point.")

When someone speaks of being "born on the cusp," that person is referring to a birth time at or near the beginning or the end of an astrological sign. For example, if you were born on August 22, you were born on the cusp of Virgo, the sign that begins on August 23. Indeed, depending on what year you were born, your birth time might even be in the first degree of Virgo. People born on the very day a sign begins or ends are often confused about what sign they really are—a confusion made more complicated by the fact that the Sun does not move into or out of a sign at *exactly* the same moment (or even day) each year. There are slight time differences from year to year. Therefore, if you are a Leo born on July 23 or August 22, you'll find great clarity consulting a computer chart that tells you exactly where the Sun was at the very moment you were born.

As for what span of time constitutes being born on the cusp, the astrological community holds various opinions. Some astrologers claim *cusp* means being born only within the first two days or last two days of a sign (though many say this is too narrow a time frame). Others say it can be as much as within the first ten days or last ten days of a sign (which many say is too wide an interpretation). The consensus is that you were born on the cusp if your birthday is within the first *five* days or last *five* days of a sign.

The question hanging over cusp-born people is, "What sign am I really?" They feel they straddle the border of two different

*In a birth chart, a cusp is also the point at which an astrological House begins.

countries. To some extent, this is true. If you were born on the cusp, you're under the influence of both signs. However, much like being a traveler leaving one country and crossing into another, you must actually *be* in one country—you can't be in two countries at the same time. One sign is always a stronger influence, and that sign is almost invariably the sign that the Sun was actually in (in other words, your Sun sign). The reason I say "almost" is that in rare cases a chart may be so heavily weighted with planets in a certain sign that the person more keenly feels the influence of that specific sign.

For example, I have a client who was born in the evening on August 22. On that evening, the Sun was leaving Leo and entering Virgo. At the moment of her birth the Sun was still in Leo, so technically speaking she is a Leo. However, the Sun was only a couple hours away from being in Virgo, and this person has the Moon, Mercury, and Venus all in Virgo. She has always felt like a Virgo and always behaved as a Virgo.

This, obviously, is an unusual case. Generally, the Sun is the most powerful planetary influence in a chart. Even if you were born with the Sun on the very tip of the first or last degree of Leo, Leo is your Sun sign—and this is the sign you will most feel like.

Still, the influence of the approaching sign or of the sign just ending is present, and you will probably sense that mixture in yourself.

BORN JULY 23 THROUGH JULY 27

You are Leo with Cancer tendencies. You have high aspirations and tend to be creative, and at the same time you are methodical and studious. You want to make the "right" decisions and hate to be caught unprepared or off guard. Mental work stimulates you; you have good powers of concentration and an ability to express yourself. Because of your ebullience and warmth, you attract many friends. You are often extravagant with money because you love to buy beautiful things. You also are headstrong and possessive in love.

BORN AUGUST 18 THROUGH AUGUST 22

You are Leo with Virgo tendencies. You gain attention because of your strong personality and sense of style. Determination is one of your dominant qualities; you climb over obstacles to reach a goal or get something your heart is set on. You have a taste for elegance and like to travel first class. Though you are very level-headed when analyzing other people's problems, you are basically an emotional person. You make decisions first with your heart and then rationalize with your head.

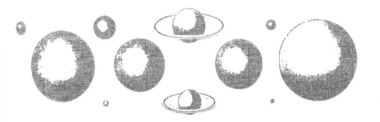

YOUR SPECIAL DAY OF BIRTH

JULY 23

You have depth, passion, and an ocean of feelings—and are also a bold Leo adventurer. With your mix of unconventional creativity and a conservative approach to money, you have a talent for business. In love, you're a wild romantic who needs lots of sexy cuddling.

JULY 24

You're highly individualistic and somewhat zany, yet dependable and extremely loyal. Highly intelligent, you're an insatiable learner. Romantically, you've had to live through a painful experience to learn how worthy you are.

JULY 25

On the surface, you're communicative and outgoing, but inwardly you keep your secrets. Only with time are you able to trust enough to reveal your true self. You have an instinct for making money. In love, you are very passionate and very vulnerable.

JULY 26

You are sensitive and refined, quick-witted and expressive—a complicated bundle of intelligence and artistry. You have a touch of the poet in you and also a brilliant eye for commerce. Emotionally, you can be very steadfast for someone who loves the real you.

JULY 27

With your delightful sense of humor, people don't always take you seriously. But you're ambitious and goal oriented, and stronger than you know. You won't do anything cheaply. In love, you can be a creature of fantasy and must learn not to let your judgment be clouded by illusion.

JULY 28

You seem unpredictable because you're restless and have unconventional tastes, but you're capable of bold and daring action once you commit to an objective. You're extremely intuitive emotionally, and never dishonest in love. In relationships, your intensity can cause you pain.

JULY 29

You're a great communicator and know how to accept responsibility. Therefore, you're often given a lot to handle. Your life's purpose, though, is to be creative; this is what keeps you sane. You're affectionate and love with all your heart, yet also a flirt. You can't help it.

JULY 30

You have dazzling talents and fantastic dreams—and enough stamina to go the distance. But you're a maverick who goes your own way because you hate deadlines and interference. In love relationships, you're passionate and impulsive, yet you crave peace and security.

JULY 31

You have deep devotion, yet you're an enigma, for you seem eccentric and aloof. Actually, you're independent and have self-belief, and don't live your life according to what others want of you. In love, you give yourself wholly to your relationships, of which there will be many.

AUGUST 1

You're an observer, philosopher, and muse, and a role model to many. Privately, you constantly question yourself, but publicly you're confident and charismatic. In love, you need mental affinity and much physical affection. It takes someone special to match you emotionally and intellectually.

AUGUST 2

You're an entertainer along with being an expert; people come to you for advice. Yet lurking beneath your surface are complicated feelings that you'll spend a lifetime sorting out. Love can be elusive, for you're hard to get to know, though your destiny is to find happiness.

AUGUST 3

You're genial, genuine, and very easy to get along with. Inside, you burn with ambitions and desires—and impatience to get to your goals. In time, you come to see that when you're in charge, without interference, you're on the right path. In love, your passions also burn intensely.

AUGUST 4

You're a freedom-loving explorer, and at the same time a shrewd businessperson who can create an empire from the germ of an idea. You were born to make a mark on the world. You have powerful emotions that you must learn to trust; usually it's only in hindsight that you see how much you were loved.

AUGUST 5

High-flying, energetic, and with great people-pizzazz, you burst onto every scene filled with ideas. You're able to bring others into harmony. The only two things to work on are your stick-to-it-iveness and, with love partners, really listening instead of trying to control.

AUGUST 6

You have a practical side—and also the side that can get lost in fantasy. These conflicting energies give you a quirky, oddball demeanor. People see you as something of a genius. You have passionate courage, but should try to curb your tendency to pick lovers who need rescuing.

AUGUST 7

Underneath your air of self-assurance, you carry the memories of painful struggles. Yet your experiences have created someone resilient, wise, caring, and deeply creative. You have the spark of greatness. In relationships, you shine, but you also need to practice love of yourself.

AUGUST 8

You're polished and elegant, and you have superb social skills. Oddly, you consider yourself a loner, but you have great power with large groups of people. Be thankful for your insecurities; they keep you humble. Sexually, you're a tinderbox. Emotionally, you have difficulty trusting.

AUGUST 9

Your irrepressible spirit has served you well through dark moments. You're the one others call on in a crisis, and your personal power will also ensure victory in a major life enterprise. Love and sex tend to be problematic, for you want to care for and control a lover but really need someone strong.

AUGUST 10

You're intuitive and adaptable, and famous for your ability to integrate with others. Yet you need a lot of space in which to do your own thing. You have a rich imagination and can accomplish unique creative work. Your lessons in love are about not making lovers dependent on you.

AUGUST 11

You have an independent mind and strong opinions, and are known as a character. You also have unusual performing talent. You're reluctant to take emotional risks in love because you feel vulnerable, yet in love you've made incredibly bold leaps following your heart.

AUGUST 12

You're a bundle of pent-up energy—and undeniable star quality. You're compelling, have eclectic tastes, and, because people trust you, have a knack for ferreting out valuable career information. Your passion can be overwhelming to a lover, but under the volcano beats a gentle heart.

AUGUST 13

You are fun-loving, extravagant, the life of the party. Your magical way with people is useful in your career; you know how to make things happen. You have powerful emotions, especially those of love and passion. Learn to express yourself—you have a tendency to block anger.

AUGUST 14

You have a brilliant intellect and strong ethics, and can be obsessive about small details. You resist ties that bind, yet are superdevoted. When someone has a problem, your first instinct is to help. Your fiery qualities are ignited in sexual relationships—sex usually leads to love, not the other way around.

AUGUST 15

You're a private person, but don't seem so. Others see your strength and resilience, and your off-the-wall creativity. Emotionally, though, if someone becomes too dependent you back away; you can be aloof. However, with the lover who captures your soul, you're devoted forever.

AUGUST 16

You have a cutting-edge mind. People want your take on the latest, newest, and best. You seem lucky, but luck actually comes because you're a hard worker with diligent follow-through. You're a sexy love partner—but need to guard against arousing jealousy with your flirtatious ways.

AUGUST 17

Upsetting the status quo is your forte—you're a charming rebel who actually makes things work better. You have street smarts, inventiveness, and a wild creative streak. Emotionally, you're complicated. You require a lover who can put up with both your intensity and your need for space.

AUGUST 18

When it comes to taking responsibility and getting things done, you're a heavyweight. At the same time, you have a lightheartedness people can't resist. You're highly intelligent and deeply honest. In romantic affairs, your life is like a soap opera because you're so enticing.

AUGUST 19

Your mercury-quick mind is filled with innovative ideas. And because you have the courage to be different, you can actually bring your plans to fruition. You're good at long-term friendship, but in love you have a way of getting into unconventional romantic entanglements.

AUGUST 20

You're a brilliant, determined achiever with a wildly independent streak. You like adventure and having your own way. You're fearless, sophisticated, and destined to become famous among your peers. In love, you have a truthful, committed heart, yet you're also a wanderer.

AUGUST 21

You're stubborn but easy to deal with because you tell the truth. You don't seek the limelight but nevertheless have high visibility because you're original. People copy your style. In love, you're an old-fashioned romantic wrapped up in a body made for passionate sex.

AUGUST 22

You're receptive and sensitive, and at the same time daring, ambitious, and in possession of a brilliant mind. You have great inner strength that will see you through anything. You can be cool and rational in making decisions—but in love you're deeply emotional and can be a sacrificer.

YOU AND CHINESE ASTROLOGY

With Marco Polo's adventurous travels in A.D. 1275, Europeans learned for the first time of the great beauty, wealth, history, and romance of China. Untouched as they were by outside influences, the Chinese developed their astrology along different lines from other ancient cultures, such as the Egyptians, Babylonians, and Greeks in whose traditions Western astrology has its roots. Therefore the Chinese zodiac differs from the zodiac of the West. To begin with, it's based on a lunar cycle rather than Western astrology's solar cycle. The Chinese zodiac is divided into twelve years, and each year is represented by a different animal—the rat, ox, tiger, rabbit, dragon, snake, horse, goat, monkey, rooster, dog, or pig. The legend of the twelve animals is that when Buddha lay on his deathbed, he asked the animals of the forest to come and bid him farewell. These twelve were the first to arrive. The cat, as the story goes, is not among the animals because it was napping and couldn't be bothered to make the journey. (In some Asian countries, however, such as Vietnam, the cat replaces the rabbit.)

Like Western astrology, in which the zodiac signs have different characteristics, each of the twelve Chinese animal years assigns character traits specific to a person born in that year. For example, the Year of the Rat confers honesty and an analytical mind, whereas the Year of the Monkey grants charm and a quick ability to spot opportunity.

Here are descriptions for Leo for each Chinese animal year:

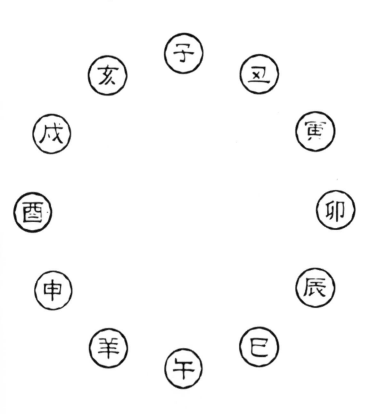

Years of the Rat

1900	1960	2020	2080
1912	1972	2032	2092
1924	1984	2044	
1936	1996	2056	
1948	2008	2068	

Unlike the West's downbeat view of the rat, in China the Rat is lively, amusing, communicative, full of charm, and a joy to be associated with. Rat natives are said to be lovers of pleasure and fun, gambling and games of luck, and good food, which certainly aligns with Leo enjoyments. As a Leo Rat you're doubly blessed with exuberance and magnetism—and a special light in your heart. At the same time, you have strong backbone, are extremely honest, and take pride in what you do. The Year of the Rat underlines an independent streak. Unlike many Leos, you don't overconcern yourself with what others think of you. You, however, can be far too meddling and bossy with people, and you *are* an opportunist. Still, when you love someone, you're generous, sentimental, sexually passionate, and very loyal. Compatible partners are born in the Years of the Monkey, Pig, Rat, and Snake.

Years of the Ox

1901	1961	2021	2081
1913	1973	2033	2093
1925	1985	2045	
1937	1997	2057	
1949	2009	2069	

In the Asian zodiac, the Ox is considered a strong, loyal, tenacious leader. Contrary to being lumbering, the Ox is in fact refined, stylish, elegant, and eloquent. These special "cream of the crop" Ox qualities blend beautifully with your Leo radiance and magnetism. In a word, you're *inspiring*. You encourage others to live up to their best potential, usually by example. You're neither a fly-by-night nor jack-of-all-trades. Leo Ox is a specialist, an expert in an important subject. You put effort into creating stability—your way of insuring you're free enough to do creative work and live gracefully without worry about scraping by. Negatively, you do have a temper, can be rigid and ultrastubborn, and are authoritarian—Leo traits emphasized by the Year of the Ox. In romantic affairs, you're captivated by sex. You also love deeply and offer faith and commitment. Compatible partners are born in the Years of the Rabbit, Rooster, Monkey, Pig, and Snake.

IF YOU ARE LEO BORN IN THE YEAR OF THE TIGER

Years of the Tiger

1902	1962	2022	2082
1914	1974	2034	2094
1926	1986	2046	
1938	1998	2058	
1950	2010	2070	

In Chinese astrology, the Tiger symbolizes bravery and a noble spirit. The Tiger is magnetic, extremely bold, an impetuous innovator, and always in the lead. Tiger qualities marry perfectly to Leo traits—a Leo Tiger exudes an air of authority, a colorful persona, and great fervor. You live life on a quest to find the magnificent destiny you were meant to achieve. The Year of the Tiger ushers in disruption, and you're a revolutionary. In career, you love the "big idea" and running your own show. You don't follow orders, and definitely can be selfish and short-tempered. But you work like a demon. Love is always a many-splendored thing—it's in romantic affairs you discover how passionate and possessive you are, how fiercely you commit. You're extremely sexual and must learn good judgment. Compatible partners are born in the Years of the Rabbit, Dog, Dragon, Monkey, Pig, and Tiger.

IF YOU ARE LEO BORN IN THE YEAR OF THE RABBIT

Years of the Rabbit

1903	1963	2023	2083
1915	1975	2035	2095
1927	1987	2047	
1939	1999	2059	
1951	2011	2071	

The Asian Rabbit is not at all timorous or timid. More like Bugs Bunny, the Rabbit is wily, amusing, talkative, and theatrical. Chinese texts speak fondly of the Rabbit's adaptability and talent for landing on its feet. Rabbit charm and quick-wittedness energize your Leo ability to seize the spotlight. As a Leo Rabbit, you have extra star quality—you're imaginative, creative, and generously endowed with talent, and you have wonderful potential for greatness. Difficulties arise when your vanity and arrogance get overblown, but you do have humor and a compelling way with people. In love you can be jealous, and in sex obsessive. Lovers often mistake this for commitment, which poses problems. You have issues with trust, and it takes time to truly give your heart for keeps. Compatible partners are born in the Years of the Goat, Dog, Dragon, Snake, Horse, and Monkey.

IF YOU ARE LEO BORN IN THE YEAR OF THE DRAGON

辰

Years of the Dragon

1904	1964	2024	2084
1916	1976	2036	2096
1928	1988	2048	
1940	2000	2060	
1952	2012	2072	

In China, the Dragon is a divine and splendid beast symbolizing good fortune and immense power. Among the Dragon's qualities are intelligence, perseverance, and the realization of dreams. Being born in the Year of the Dragon confers honor; Chinese folklore teaches that Dragons are gifted and ambitious, and pursue their objectives with great force. As a Leo, you're already endowed with ability to influence people and a special gift for setting trends. Putting Dragon passion into the mix makes you even more creative and flamboyant. Innovative ideas just fly into your head, and you have an instinct for finding venues in which your super-talents shine. You are vain, to be sure, but incapable of meanness. Love is often a bumpy road, for you give yourself unreservedly but expect a relationship to fill all your needs. You're bound to suffer disillusionment. Compatible partners are born in the Years of the Rabbit, Goat, Monkey, Snake, and Tiger.

IF YOU ARE LEO BORN IN THE YEAR OF
THE SNAKE

Ⓔ

Years of the Snake

1905	1965	2025	2085
1917	1977	2037	2097
1929	1989	2049	
1941	2001	2061	
1953	2013	2073	

The Eastern Snake is a mysterious, all-knowing Goddess linked to Love, Beauty, and the Sea. In the West the snake suffers from bad press, but to the Chinese Snakes are wise, beautiful, intuitive, and sensual. Being born in the Year of the Snake endows you with fluency of expression that, added to your Leo ability to capture an audience, gives you double charisma. You have special skill for business and making money grow. You're an advice giver as well as a mover and shaker who can carve out a unique creative career. It's true you're a master manipulator who can be selfish and cunning, but the upside is you're intensely focused. Your love life is often in turmoil. You have deep feelings, but your high sex drive pulls you into side paths. You have problems, too, with possessiveness and jealousy. Compatible partners are born in the Years of the Rabbit, Rooster, Dragon, Horse, Ox, and Rat.

IF YOU ARE LEO BORN IN THE YEAR OF THE HORSE

Years of the Horse

1906	1966	2026	2086
1918	1978	2038	2098
1930	1990	2050	
1942	2002	2062	
1954	2014	2074	

Magnificent, tempestuous, and symbolizing freedom of action, the Chinese Horse is driven by its superiority. In fact, the Year of the Horse is such a significant time to be born that in Asia pregnancies are planned around it. The Horse's wildness propels it to strike out on its own. This quality of pulling away from the pack blends with your hot-blooded Leo courage, making you a person filled with desire. You're ambitious and superintelligent, and you can navigate through any challenge—in business, creative work, social situations, and foreign travel. You're a pragmatist (and a bit of a hustler), and a dreamer of big dreams. In love, you're passionate, a grand romantic, but tend to choose partners who can't live up to your expectations. In time, your heart will finally come to peace. Compatible partners are born in the Years of the Rabbit, Rooster, Goat, Horse, and Snake.

IF YOU ARE LEO BORN IN THE YEAR OF THE GOAT ✿

Years of the Goat

1907	1967	2027	2087
1919	1979	2039	2099
1931	1991	2051	
1943	2003	2063	
1955	2015	2075	

In Asian culture, the Goat is the thinker and the sage. Being born in the Year of the Goat bestows inventiveness and far vision. In Chinese tales, the Goat has charming sweetness and an air of naiveté that belies the brilliant workings of its mind. Goat imagination and ingenuity combine with your Leo creativity to bring a touch of the "mad genius." You can be undisciplined and impractical—and you're never quite satisfied—but your work has such originality, you definitely make your mark. You're an individual with great style, and can be a daredevil. Much of your emotional energy goes into others—friends, lovers, and family—and romantically you have profound capacity for attachment. You're fond of sexual experimentation, but only with the one you love. Compatible partners are born in the Years of the Rabbit, Dragon, Horse, Monkey, and Pig.

IF YOU ARE LEO BORN IN THE YEAR OF THE MONKEY

Years of the Monkey

1908	1968	2028	2088
1920	1980	2040	2100
1932	1992	2052	
1944	2004	2064	
1956	2016	2076	

The Monkey is adored in Asia for its merriment, curiosity, and ability to chase away boredom. In Japanese mythology, the Monkey accompanied the God of Travel to provide friendship and amusement. As a Leo you talk fast, walk fast, and think fast, and Monkey sparkle and vivacity only accentuate your ability to excite the public. You have great theatricality, a remarkable memory, and a knack for ferreting out information—qualities that ensure professional success. You're sincere, although when stressed known to gloss over the truth. You're adept at covering up your feelings; and emotionally, you *are* complicated. In love, you want passion and magic—indeed, you strive to feel deeply—but you tend to be controlling and changeable. After many lessons, your wandering heart will find its way home. Compatible partners are born in the Years of the Rabbit, Dragon, Ox, Pig, Rat, and Tiger.

IF YOU ARE LEO BORN IN THE YEAR OF THE ROOSTER

酉

Years of the Rooster

1909	1957	2005	2053
1921	1969	2017	2065
1933	1981	2029	2077
1945	1993	2041	2089

Chinese mythology teaches that the Rooster rescued the Sun goddess, and therefore symbolizes courage. The Rooster is feisty, outspoken, brilliant, and resourceful. The Year of the Rooster always ushers in new confidence—and born under its influence, you have extra get-up-and-go in your buoyant Leo energy. You seek out novel experiences, you're attractive and communicative, and when you speak others listen. Some people think you're brazen, but you have true boldness to your character and will always give a new venture a try. You resist discouragement and are a joy to know. With your multiplicity of talents, you're destined for fame. In love, you're sentimental and giving, and may give up too much of yourself to keep a lover. You need to learn balance. Compatible partners are born in the Years of the Horse, Ox, and Snake.

Years of the Dog

1910	1958	2006	2054
1922	1970	2018	2066
1934	1982	2030	2078
1946	1994	2042	2090

In Asia, the Dog has always symbolized fidelity. Like the real-life animal, the Dog is constant and heroic—and being born in the Year of the Dog places the mantle of duty on your shoulders. As a Leo you're already an ambitious initiator, so adding Dog tenacity to your Leo drive makes you adept at embracing huge undertakings from which others would shrink. You're a rescuer who takes responsibility for fixing what's wrong and setting the world right. In your zeal, you often forget to take care of yourself. Certainly you are your own most demanding critic. Others see a lovable charmer with superior skills who's miles ahead in the achievement department. You have a nose for sniffing out opportunity. Love is your strong suit; here is where your devotion is most visible. Once you give your heart, nothing can sway your affections. Compatible partners are born in the Years of the Rabbit, Dog, Pig, and Tiger.

Years of the Pig

1911	1959	2007	2055
1923	1971	2019	2067
1935	1983	2031	2079
1947	1995	2043	2091

In the West the pig is lowly, but in China it is held in high esteem. The Pig is gallant, warm, cultured, and knowledgeable, and made of noble character. Paired with your Leo magnetism—the fascination you generate—you can't help but appear to be lit from within. As a Leo Pig, you're an intellectual, a connoisseur in your tastes, a hard worker at your craft, and a generous friend. A fatal flaw might be the fact that you're fond of excess (too much is never enough), but you're a magnanimous sharer. In the world of business, you make important decisions without waffling, and in artistic pursuits you find your deepest fulfillment. You have amazing creativity. In love, you're a voluptuary who lives for romantic passion. You revel in good sex, lots of affection, creature comforts. Compatible partners are born in the Years of the Rabbit, Dog, Pig, and Tiger.

YOU AND NUMEROLOGY

Numerology is the language of numbers. It is the belief that there is a correlation between numbers and living things, ideas, and concepts. Certainly, numbers surround and infuse our lives (e.g., twenty-four hours in a day, twelve months of the year, etc.). And from ancient times mystics have taught that numbers carry a *vibration*, a deeper meaning that defines how each of us fits into the universe. According to numerology, you are born with a personal number that contains information about who you are and what you need to be happy. This number expresses what numerology calls your life path.

All numbers reduce to one of nine digits, numbers 1 through 9. Your personal number is based on your date of birth. To calculate your number, write your birth date in numerals. As an example, the birth date of July 28, 1983, is written 7-28-1983. Now begin the addition: 7 + 28 + 1 + 9 + 8 + 3 = 56; 56 reduces to 5 + 6 = 11; 11 reduces to 1 + 1 = 2. The personal number for someone born July 29, 1983, is *Two*.

IF YOU ARE A LEO ONE

Keywords: Confidence and Creativity

One is the number of leadership and new beginnings. You rush into whatever engages your heart—whether a new plan, a love affair, or just finding more pleasure. You're courageous and inventive, and people respond to your decisiveness if not always to your dominating ways. You're attracted to unusual pursuits because you like to be one-of-a-kind. You can't bear to be under the thumb of other people's whims and agendas. Careers that call to you are those in which you are in charge and able to work independently. As for love, you want ecstasy and passion, and the most exciting part of a flirtation is the beginning.

IF YOU ARE A LEO TWO

Keywords: Cooperation and Balance

Two is the number of cooperation and creating a secure entity. Being a Two gives you extra Leo magnetism—you attract what you need. Your magic is not only your people skills, but your ability to breathe life into empty forms (e.g., a concept, an ambitious business idea, a new relationship) and produce something of worth. In your work, you're a perfectionist—and because you have both a creative side *and* a practical side, you're drawn to careers that combine a business sense with an artistic challenge. In love, your deepest desire is for a loving partnership with someone you can trust and share confidences with.

IF YOU ARE A LEO THREE

Keywords: Expression and Sensitivity

Three symbolizes self-expression. Being a Three doubly emphasizes your Leo gift for words and a talent for visualization. You link people together so that they benefit from each other. You stimulate others to think. Because you're a connector, you're much loved as a leader, spokesperson, and friend. In a career, creativity and innovation are your specialties. You're a quick study, mentally active, and are curious about the new. In love, you need someone who excites you intellectually and sensually, and understands your complex personality. Casual acquaintances may not see your depth, but in love you must have a soulmate who does.

IF YOU ARE A LEO FOUR

Keywords: Stability and Process

Four is the number of dedication and loyalty. It represents *foundation*, exactly as a four-sided square does. You are a builder, and the direction you go in is up. First you plan, then you add the next step, the next layer. You create Leo stability by following a process, and your strength is that you're persistent. Therefore, you're able to control your environment, accomplish great works, and achieve high honor. In love, you look for a relationship with staying power. You need a faithful, giving, and understanding lover with whom you can express your rich sensuality—you're an imaginative and generous lover.

IF YOU ARE A LEO FIVE

Keywords: Freedom and Discipline

Five is the number of change and freedom. With your chameleon intellect (it can go in any direction) and charismatic ability to deal with people, you're a marvelous *persuader*. You charm and influence others, and have great skill with the public. You enjoy being a performer. Also you can visualize and, as a Five, you're the Leo best able to make new starts. You don't become stuck, and you know how to let go of what doesn't work. In love, you need romantic fantasy but also want a partner who looks ahead to new goals. When you give your heart away it's to someone with whom you passionately mesh—body and mind.

IF YOU ARE A LEO SIX

Keywords: Vision and Acceptance

Six is the number of teaching, healing, and utilizing your talents. You're geared toward changing the world or at least fixing other people's lives. Being an advice-giver and even a therapist to your friends comes naturally. You're also competitive, exacting, and demanding—especially with yourself. You have a passion to use your sharp intellect and want to be recognized for your excellence. You hold yourself up to high standards. In love, the most important ingredient is trust. You look for profound emotional involvement, yearn for total abandon, and your specialty is erotic touch.

IF YOU ARE A LEO SEVEN

Keywords: Trust and Openness

Seven is the number of the mystic and the intensely focused specialist. You have an instinct for problem-solving, and in a flash understand how things work (in business, between people, etc.). You're an intellectual, a philosopher and, in matters of style and taste, a superb judge. With your Leo ability to take charge, you carve out your own territory. Your work, though, is only part of a deeper search for trust in yourself. At your core you're extremely loyal and intensely loving, though very selective about relationships. In love, your deepest need is for a partner who can help you in your journey to becoming the real you.

IF YOU ARE A LEO EIGHT

Keywords: Abundance and Power

Eight is the number of mastery and authority. You are intelligent, alert, quick in action, born to take power in your own hands and guide traffic into the direction you want. You work well in large groups because you see what's needed and can delegate (a major success tool). Others sense you're the one who knows best, and they're right. You think big, tackle the hard stuff, and never let anyone down. As a Leo Eight, you're totally true to your word and fixed in your loyalty. Giving your promise in love is a very serious act. You are a protective and deeply caring lover, and in turn you need to know your lover is your unwavering ally.

IF YOU ARE A LEO NINE

Keywords: Integrity and Wisdom

Nine is the path of the "old soul," the number of completion and full bloom. Because it's the last number, it sums up the highs and lows of human experience, and you live a life of dramatic events. You're very intellectual and interested in all kinds of new learning—as well as deeply feeling and extremely protective. People see you as colorful and heroic because you have an adventurous outlook but are also spiritual and altruistic. In love, you're truthful and sincere—and a romantic, highly sensual creature. As a Leo Nine you generously give of yourself, often to the point of being sacrificing.

LAST WORD: YOUR LEO
UNFINISHED BUSINESS

Psychologists often use the phrase *unfinished business* to describe
unresolved issues—for example, patterns from childhood that
cause unhappiness, anger that keeps one stuck, scenarios of family dysfunction that repeat through second and third generations
(such as alcoholism or abusive behavior).

Astrology teaches that the past is indeed very much with us in
the present. And that using astrological insights can help us move
out of emotional darkness into greater clarity. Even within this
book (which is not a tome of hundreds of pages) you have read of
many of the superlatives and challenges of being Leo. You have
breathtaking gifts, and at the same time certain tendencies that
can undermine utilizing these abilities.

In nature, a fascinating fact is that in jungles and forests a
poisonous plant will grow in a certain spot, and always just a few
feet away is a plant that is the antidote to that specific poison.
Likewise, in astrology, the antidote is right there, ready to be used
when the negatives threaten to overwhelm your life.

Leo's unfinished business has to do with the focus on self. Whatever you interact with becomes an extension of *you*. You have difficulty seeing past yourself. You're the center, the point of concentration, the cosmology of one.

Like the other two Fire signs (Aries and Sagittarius), you have a shining quality, a radiance that comes from within. Leo is the sign of self, and you have strong self-awareness. For as long as you can remember, you've longed to see a perfect you reflected in the eyes of others. You crave approval, attention, and love because in this you see how important and special you are. You want to be adored for your light.

Certainly, you have much to adore. You're exciting, inspirational, talented—an initiator of activity, brimming with life. You're a gleeful child who spontaneously says yes and brings joy to others. You're idealistic, generous, cheerful; your positive attitude makes wonderful things happen.

The problem is that your intense desire for validation, your self-absorption, causes you suffering. It isn't the fact you are interested in yourself (all human beings are self-oriented). Your pain comes from not getting *enough* feedback that you're wonderful. Of course, there never is enough. If you're not seen as brilliant and splendid, you feel embarrassed and mediocre. At times, your need to be outstanding can create a stumbling block of avoidance—you'll find excuses not to begin an undertaking because you must be matchless and are afraid you won't be.

Somehow alongside your generosity, your warmth, your understanding heart and ability to love, you tend to operate as a cosmos of one. You have difficulty relinquishing center stage; you overdramatize yourself and overdominate.

Astrology teaches that down deep Leo doesn't feel lovable, and you try too hard to build yourself up. You set impossibly high standards for yourself that essentially block you. The bumps and setbacks you inevitably encounter make you feel you're failing, and you keep fighting off disappointment and depression that cause you to try even harder to get applause from others. You're driven by an inner "beat the clock" that doesn't let up.

The strong Leo drive can negatively impact relationships with the very people who love you. Those close to you frequently have to compete against your ambitions. You're exhausting to keep up with and often tense and temperamental.

Yet the antidotes are there to be found in their entirety in being Leo, for you are indeed a superlative and superior person. If anyone in the zodiac can tap into tools of self-empowerment, it's Leo. You are gifted and brilliant and courageous. All you need to do to "create" yourself is to use the awesome creativity with which you were born. When you express yourself, you are living purposefully; you're being authentically Leo. Accessing your bold creativity is your means to discovering how worthy and valuable you are, how rich you are in talents—not because others tell you this but because you see yourself in your true light. When you let go of fear of failure and the pressure of performing for others, your great expectations will come to pass.

Alongside your vanity and self-exaggeration exists a golden spirit of nobility. On the highest level, Leo represents a glowing expansiveness. You among few understand the concept of possibility and how limitless life can be. Your unfinished business is to get past your ego and to open your heart to love and work—to experience passion with all your being.

FAMOUS PEOPLE WITH THE SUN IN LEO

Ben Affleck
Gracie Allen
Neil Armstrong
Lucille Ball
Antonio Banderas
Count Basie
Ethel Barrymore
Tony Bennett
Simon Bolívar
Napoleon Bonaparte
Barry Bonds
Ray Bradbury
Diamond Jim Brady
Sandra Bullock
Claus von Bulow
Ken Burns
Fidel Castro
Ramond Chandler
Julia Child
Bill Clinton
Paula Creamer
Guy de Maupassant
Cecil B. DeMille
Robert De Niro
Elizabeth Dole
Madame du Barry
Marcel Duchamp
Leo Durocher

Amelia Earhart
Zelda Fitzgerald
Jerry Garcia
Frank Gifford
Kathy Lee Gifford
Jeff Gordon
Al Gore
Melanie Griffith
Mata Hari
Alfred Hitchcock
Dustin Hoffman
Whitney Houston
John Huston
Aldous Huxley
Mick Jagger
Peter Jennings
Magic Johnson
Carl Jung
Garrison Keillor
Francis Scott Key
T. E. Lawrence
Monica Lewinsky
Jennifer Lopez
Madonna
Steve Martin
Maureen McGovern
Herman Melville
Robert Mitchum

Annie Oakley
Barack Obama
Carroll O'Connor
Jacqueline Kennedy Onassis
Peter O'Toole
Dorothy Parker
Maxfield Parrish
Sean Penn
Roman Polanski
Robert Redford
Gene Roddenberry
Kenny Rogers
J. K. Rowling
Yves Saint Laurent
Pete Sampras
Arnold Schwarzenegger
George Bernard Shaw
Percy Bysshe Shelley
Kevin Spacey
Danielle Steel
Martha Stewart
Alfred, Lord Tennyson
Leon Uris
Andy Warhol
Shelley Winters
Orville Wright

PART TWO

ALL ABOUT YOUR SIGN OF LEO

LEO'S ASTROLOGICAL AFFINITIES, LINKS, AND LORE

SYMBOL: The Lion

Regal, brave, dominating, sometimes indolent. Possessing nobility and pride, and strongly associated with kingship. The Lion is the totem animal of rulers and emperors, and of gods such as Apollo and the deity Krishna. In ancient Egypt, the symbol of two lions facing away from each other represented light and dark, birth and death, past and future.

RULING PLANET: The Sun ☉

The center of our solar system, a star that burns with intense fire and supplies us with light, heat, and energy. In ancient cultures, the Sun was worshipped as the physical manifestation of a Supreme Being. Astrologically, the Sun is the most powerful planetary influence, bestowing vitality and authority. It represents the ego.

DOMINANT KEYWORD

I WILL

GLYPH ♌

The pictograph represents two valves of the human heart (a part of the anatomy that Leo rules). It also signifies the Sun (Leo's ruler) and its course through the heavens. This was an ancient pictograph for life constantly renewing itself. In addition, this is the Greek symbol for the first letter of Leo. In symbolic terms, it is two incomplete circles of the Sun joined by a crescent moon, symbolizing power derived from both the intellect and the emotions.

PART OF THE BODY RULED BY LEO:
The Back, the Spine, and the Heart

Emotional strain and physical overexertion cause back and spine ailments in Leo people. Symbolically, the back, spine, and heart represent courage and passion.

LUCKY DAY: Sunday

The day named for the Sun, ruler of Leo.

LUCKY NUMBERS: 8 and 9

Numerologically, 8 is the number of strength, confidence, authority, and mastery—and 9 is linked to creativity, achievement, and a dramatic style. These qualities align with the nature of Leo.

TAROT CARD: Strength

The card in the Tarot linked to Leo is Strength, one of the most powerful cards in the deck. An ancient name for this card is Daughter of the Flaming Sword. In the Tarot, this card signifies the taming of wild forces within oneself and bringing them into proper balance with one's spiritual nature. It speaks of finding the fortitude to commit to the positive course of action. Meanings associated with this card are staying power, zeal, vitality, and lust for life. When this card turns up in a Tarot reading, it symbolizes the strength of will to overcome problems.

The card itself pictures a woman dressed in white, bending over a lion, gently closing its mouth. The woman represents the ability to master over baser emotions (such as jealousy, anger, and spite), and to focus one's dedication and passion on doing the right thing.

For Leo, Strength says that when you have moral courage on your side, you have authority over any situation. It tells you love triumphs over hate.

MAGICAL BIRTHSTONE: Ruby

Prized for its intense crimson color (the color of vitality and passion), the ruby has been called the "lord of precious stones." The name ruby comes from the Latin word *rubens*, meaning red. This stone is a symbol of royalty. The ancients thought the ruby not only reflected light but generated light and could be seen in the dark; thus it was said to provide spiritual guidance. Historically, rubies were often laid beneath the foundation of buildings to bring good fortune to the structure. For Leo, the ruby protects against physical injury, ensures faithfulness, and brings its wearer serenity of mind. These qualities are enhanced by wearing the ruby on the left side of the body, which connects the jewel to the heart.

SPECIAL COLORS: Gold and Orange

The magnetic colors of the Sun. Gold symbolizes power, light, and life—and inherent in its color is representation of the Sun. Orange represents energy and fertility.

CONSTELLATION OF LEO

Leo is among the brightest and most easily recognizable constellations in the heavens. Down through history, this constellation has been called the Lion and identified with the Sun king. The Babylonians called Leo the Great Light, and one of the stars in this constellation, Regalus, is called both Heart of the Lion and the Little King. Ancient Egyptians worshipped the stars in Leo because at midsummer, when they were at their brightest, the Sun's journey through this constellation coincided with the annual rising of the great river Nile.

CITIES

Rome, Prague, Damascus, Los Angeles

COUNTRIES

France, Italy, Romania

FLOWERS

Sunflower and Marigold

TREES

Orange and all Citrus Trees, Palm, Olive

HERBS AND SPICES

Saffron, Peppermint, Rosemary, and Rue

METAL: Gold

Symbolizing value, power, royalty, strength, and the Sun. Gold has always signified wealth and prestige. This is one of the most precious and beautiful metals of all, and inextricably linked to the element of Fire and to the Sun. Gold is unaffected by tarnishing or corrosion, and thus emblematic of immortality. Throughout the world, gold is the standard for many monetary currencies (known as the *gold standard*). The written symbol for gold (a circle with a dot in the center) is both the astrological symbol of and Chinese character for the Sun, Leo's ruler.

ANIMALS RULED BY LEO

All felines

DANGER

The Leo personality can be bombastic and challenging, and, often unknowingly, it can provoke others into impulsive violence. Leos are also prone to being victims of slander.

PERSONAL PROVERB

The greatest source of energy is pride in what you are doing.

KEYWORDS FOR LEO

Creative and gifted

Courageous

Warmhearted and generous

Exceedingly loyal

Stylish, regal

Strong and dominant

A leader

Positive and enthusiastic

Passionate sex drive

Trusting although gullible

Self-promoting

Dramatic, showy

Big spender

Good executive

Decisive

Seeking the spotlight

Authoritative

Hates details, shirks routine

Self-indulgent

Demanding and overbearing

Looks for the big success

Vain

Thin-skinned

Narcissistic

HOW ASTROLOGY SLICES AND DICES YOUR SIGN OF LEO

DUALITY: Masculine

The twelve astrological signs are divided into two groups, *masculine* and *feminine*. Six are masculine and six are feminine; this is known as the sign's *duality*. A masculine sign is direct and energetic. A feminine sign is receptive and magnetic. These attributes were given to the signs about 2,500 years ago. Today modern astrologers avoid the sexism implicit in these distinctions. A masculine sign does not mean "positive and forceful" any more than a feminine sign means "negative and weak." In modern terminology, the masculine signs, such as your sign of Leo, are defined as outer-directed and strong through action. The feminine signs are self-contained and strong through inner reserves.

TRIPLICITY (ELEMENT): Fire

The twelve signs are also divided into groups of three signs. Each of these three-sign groups is called a *triplicity*, and each of these denotes an *element*. The elements are *Fire*, *Earth*, *Air*, and *Water*. In astrology, an element symbolizes a fundamental characterization of the sign.

The three *Fire* signs are Aries, Leo, and Sagittarius. Fire signs are active and enthusiastic.

The three *Earth* signs are Taurus, Virgo, and Capricorn. Earth signs are practical and stable.

The three *Air* signs are Gemini, Libra, and Aquarius. Air signs are intellectual and communicative.

The three *Water* signs are Cancer, Scorpio, and Pisces. Water signs are emotional and intuitive.

QUADRUPLICITY (QUALITY): Fixed

The twelve signs are also divided into groups of four signs. Each of these four-sign groups is called a *quadruplicity*, and each of these denotes a *quality*. The qualities are *Cardinal*, *Fixed*, and *Mutable*. In astrology, the quality signifies the sign's interaction with the outside world.

Four signs are *Cardinal** signs. These are Aries, Cancer, Libra, and Capricorn. Cardinal signs are enterprising and outgoing. They are the initiators and leaders.

---

*When the Sun crosses the four cardinal points in the zodiac, we mark the beginning of each of our four seasons. Aries begins spring; Cancer begins summer; Libra begins fall; Capricorn begins winter.

Four signs are *Fixed*. These are Taurus, Leo, Scorpio, and Aquarius. Fixed signs are resistant to change. They hold on; they're perfectors and finishers, rather than originators.

Four signs are *Mutable*. These are Gemini, Virgo, Sagittarius, and Pisces. Mutable signs are flexible, versatile, and adaptable. They are able to adjust to differing circumstances.

Your sign of Leo is a Masculine, Fire, Fixed sign—and no other sign in the zodiac is this exact combination. Your sign is a one-of-a-kind combination, and therefore you express the characteristics of your duality, element, and quality differently from any other sign.

For example, your sign is a *Masculine* sign, meaning you are vigorous and assertive. You're a *Fire* sign, meaning you're enthusiastic, energetic, passionate. And you're a *Fixed* sign, meaning you're loyal, determined, resistant to change, and not easily sidetracked.

Now, the sign of Aries is also Masculine and Fire; but unlike Leo (which is Fixed), Aries is Cardinal. Like you, Aries is action oriented, excitable, charismatic, and a born leader—but Aries is focused on making new beginnings. Its strongest surge of power is at the start of something new (a project, a relationship), but once things are established its enthusiasm wanes. Aries doesn't have your follow-through or stick-to-it-iveness. You, being Fixed, have fortitude and endurance. You'll utilize your tools (your organizational skills and people connections) to make an enterprise grow. Your sense of pride is tied to the success of your venture, and you'll stay and do the work until you reach your goal.

Sagittarius, too, is Masculine and Fire; but unlike Leo (which is Fixed), Sagittarius is Mutable. Like you, Sagittarius is imaginative and expressive, and has high aspirations and a generous heart. However, being Mutable, Sagittarius is easily distractible and tends to say yes to each new enticing idea. Sagittarius wastes energy trying to go in too many directions. It overpromises on its performance, and underestimates on its time—and is not known for dependability. You, being Fixed, stubbornly hang in for the long haul. Passionate determination runs through your character. You embrace whatever is needed (such as the work involved) and see it through. You have fixity of focus Sagittarius does not. In addition, your commitment is seen in your loyalty to other people.

POLARITY: Aquarius

The twelve signs are also divided into groups of two signs. Each of these two-sign groups is called a *polarity* (meaning "opposite"). Each sign in the zodiac has a polarity, which is its opposite sign in the other half of the zodiac. The two signs express opposite characteristics.

Leo and Aquarius are a polarity. Leo is the sign that governs pleasure and creativity. You look for situations and relationships in which you can express your style and taste, and shine in the center of people's attention. Leo was born to be splendid. You have a dominating personality that needs to feel special—and needs to be fed by love. Praise and admiration motivate you, and you're at your best in front of an approving audience. It's been said Leo has a strong heart physically, but a vulnerable one emotionally. You're easily hurt by neglect and absence of love.

Leo is deeply invested in relationships. You give your loyalty and expect it to be returned. A betrayal is very wounding and leaves you unsure of yourself (how could you have misplaced your trust?). Basically, Leo is emotional—it's the sign of the *heart*.

Everything you think and do and pursue starts from this glowing center.

Aquarius, your opposite sign, is the sign of aspiration, hopes, and dreams. Aquarians are loving, but they tend to put their caring and energy into creating positive change in the world (politically, within the group, etc.). They are humanists, philosophers, and reformers. They "love" at a distance, and are less interested in intensely close personal relationships than in expressing their freedom to be unique individuals. Aquarians view things from the intellect, whereas you view things from the heart. Both Leo and Aquarius are Fixed signs, but Aquarius's fixity is in ideas, and yours is in emotional connections.

Astrologically, you as a Leo can benefit from adopting some of Aquarius's detachment. Relationships, projects, your work all become an extension of *you*, and you suffer mightily if they fail you. You're greatly invested in what others think of you. You want to be babied (adored, praised, caressed), yet your demands for attention tend to be off-putting. Leo is the sign of the child and can get stuck in the "terrible twos" stage of *I want, I want*. You're often a strain to be with. By tapping into Aquarius's grown-up independence, you can spare yourself pain. Aquarius strives to be different, and you, too, can find deep satisfaction in your own creativity and intelligence—rather than depending on others for reinforcing feedback. You are the one with capacity to inspire and encourage others. And you were born to accomplish great things on your own!

In turn, Aquarius has much to learn from Leo's emotional vitality and lust for life. At the top of the list is to be able to bond with others. You have warmth that radiates outward to embrace people, and this energy lifts their spirits. Cool Aquarius keeps others at arms-length and can be unaware of emotional undercurrents. Its attention is not on the inner workings of another person. The great lesson Aquarius can take from Leo is how powerful it is to love from the heart.